BUSH TUCKERS TRAIL

BUSH-TUCKERS Challenge

This edition was first published
For Amazon in 2024 AD

Written and Conceptualised by
Roger P. Thomas MCSD

Studio contact
Rogertheartist5@gmail.com

BUSH-TUCKERS CHALLENGE PASSPORT

Your Photo

Name..
Email...
Home Patch...................................

Let Your Bush-Tuckering Begin

STEP ONE...
Start with local wasteland / grass verge

Where did you plant it ?..
What did you plant ?..
When ?..

BUSH-TUCKER Challenge 1

Your First Bush-Tuckers Target is TEN Urban Guerilla plantings and then I will illustrate a local Church of your choice

Where did you plant it ?..
What did you plant ?..
When ?...

BUSH-TUCKER Challenge 2

Where did you plant it ?..
What did you plant ?...
When ?...

BUSH-TUCKER Challenge **3**

Day Three of EDEN

Raspberry

Raspberries, Loganberries, Tayberries and Youngberries are cane fruits.

They can also, when grown, provide a screen for unmentionables or hide vegetable plots.

Raspberries can be eaten immediately or frozen for dessert.

Raspberries can be supported on 6-8 foot posts with horizontal wires between them.

Plant 18 inches apart.

Cut canes down in February and cut out fruited expired canes as they appear.

Add manure and compost in spring.

Do not hoe around roots, they are fragile.

Replant runner off-shoots, which will appear all the time.

Within ten years, three plants could easily give you one hundred bushes.

For those of you who are gardeners, replant these runners from your own garden, and present these in pots to your local Church. Let's force the issue. Put with it a note to the Vicar, photocopying whole chapter.

I give permission for you to photocopy this whole chapter to give with plants.
Roger P. Thomas MCSD.

Day Three of EDEN

Blackberry Cloche

Blackberries bear long arching branches which can actually be trained on horizontal wires between 8 foot high posts.

Or, using an old gazebo, perhaps a little worse for wear, approx 9' x 9' square, and with a hacksaw, you can easily make it a 9' x 1' oblong structure, then cover it with chicken wire, peg down securely, or add secondary vertical posts at each end to give it strength if wind is a problem in that area, and plant three Blackberry Brambles in a line, inside the structure. The Brambles can be left to grow wild.

A sign can be added.

"To all, please cut protruding shoots between November and June."

The gazebo is about six feet high, which might need the use of a step ladder occasionally.

Fruit should be available July to September.

Great to add to cooked apples, or a handful in that morning porridge.

Where did you plant it ?..
What did you plant ?...
When ?..

BUSH-TUCKER Challenge | **4**

Stop sitting on the fence
What was your experience like ?

....

....

....

....

....

....

....

....

....

....

....

....

Where did you plant it ?..
What did you plant ?...
When ?...

BUSH-TUCKER Challenge **5**

Where did you plant it ?..
What did you plant ?..
When ?..

BUSH-TUCKER Challenge **6**

Day Three of EDEN

Apple

As an experiment, I cut one foot long new growth branches, cut at base across, not diagonally, with a leaf at the top, then dipped it into rooting compound, placed six in a bucket of compost, kept moist, in fact God watered them throughout the winter, so I did nothing after that, then next autumn, half of them started sprouting leaves, probably another year and they will be strong enough to plant out, I cut about twenty branches from old apple trees in the area, the trees on the roadside, with nearly half the branches sprouting.

This is not an instant fruit bearing exercise, expect fruit between five to ten years, this is a plan ahead project, start now.

Apple trees can be trained into Bush, Pyramid, Cordon, Espalier and Fan, the last three require posts and wires. The first three normally bear fruit earlier, after five years.

Do not grass over the roots for the first two years, the soil needs a lot of moisture.

Plant trees around eight metres apart.

It is an old Celtic tradition, which I kept with my Great-Nephew Kyle, to cut out old and dead branches on Christmas Eve, perhaps this can be turned into an annual event, and don't forget the Wassailing annual celebrations in January. Any excuse for a party.

Plum has a very similar set up, perhaps with space you could set up an apple-apple-plum-apple-apple row.

Day Three of EDEN

CHERRY

Cherry trees grow about forty feet high and are ideal for parks and large Church grounds, they are very colourful.

To access the fruit you will be in direct competition with the birds, so fruit needs to be collected as soon as it is ripe.

To collect the fruit, cut cherries with a secateur as pulling the branch can damage the branches for future fruiting.

All cherries are sweet except Morello which is sour.

Fruiting is generally June and July, except Morello which is later, until September.

The Cherry tree will need a pollinating partner nearby.

There are new dwarf cherry trees for easy fruit picking.

To propagate, cut one foot long new branches, with a top leaf, dip in rooting compound, and plant in moist compost in the autumn.

Cherry Trees may be a good distraction to keep the birds away from other fruits nearby.

Where did you plant it ?..
What did you plant ?..
When ?..

BUSH-TUCKER Challenge 7

Where did you plant it ?..
What did you plant ?..
When ?...

BUSH-TUCKER Challenge

8

Where did you plant it ?..
What did you plant ?...
When ?...

BUSH-TUCKER Challenge **9**

Day Three of EDEN

Sweet Chestnut

Sweet Chestnuts were brought to Britain by the Romans.

They are a Mediteranean tree.

These need large areas, please cut down those sycamore and replace with Sweet Chestnut.

Sweet Chestnuts can be grown from branch cuttings, but why bother, the seed if planted properly, will produce a 90% sapling success rate.

Get the Council to plant them in all their parks, create saplings yourself and offer them free.

Sweet chestnuts can be eaten cold, or roasted, or pureed for stuffing chickens and turkey.

Why not have a sweet chestnut tree in the Church grounds, crop and have a Roasted chestnut and carol evening.

Day Three of EDEN

Hazel

Here's a thought, every Farm hedge in Britain should be a hazel hedge.

Certainly Church hedges and borders could easily be hazelnut producers.

Hazel is a doddle, just cut a branch and stick it in, most catch, great for garden and churchyard screening.

Squirrel, woodpecker and dormouse heaven.

Hazel has a reputation as a magical tree, protects you against evil spirits, this has got to be a good reason to plant in a Churchyard.

Hazel is a source of food, medicine and materials.

It is great for carbon capture.

It's only predator or disease problem is being damaged by Deer, oh, dear.

Hazel has also got rooted off-shoots at the base, which can be immediately replanted.

Do you like Nutella spread- check out the ingredients.

Important to me- Hazel was my Mum's name. That was clearly a Godwink of the highest order, a nudge throughout my life.

Where did you plant it ?...
What did you plant ?..
When ?..

BUSH-TUCKER Challenge | **10**

For reaching TEN plantings
I will now create a sketch of YOUR local
Manor House gardens or Pub.
All I require is the name of the building and
£35 to cover research, postage and packing.
You can then use this design on mugs,
t-shirts, even duvet covers, simply create a
free Zazzle account.
Or just simply print it off and frame it for
your own very potting shed.
Congratulations

Oldway Mansion

Where did you plant it ?..
What did you plant ?..
When ?...

BUSH-TUCKER Challenge

11

Where did you plant it?..
What did you plant?...
When?..

BUSH-TUCKER Challenge

12

Day Three of EDEN

RHUBARB

Do not eat Rhubarb leaves, cut at churchyard, leave the leaves in Church compost area.

Use the leaves as a natural pesticide, to protect roses, fruit, vegetables and herbs.
To make- boil 1 kg of Rhubarb LEAVES in two litres of water for 30 minutes. Strain and add 125 g of biodegradable washing detergent powder. Mix until powder is dissolved. Leave to cool and spray on as desired using a pump action spray bottle. LEAVE at least two weeks before picking any fruit that has been sprayed. Wash food well before eating.

Rhubarb is generally available to crop from April to July.

Each Rhubarb plant can yield up to 5 lbs of produce.

Difficult to store.

Eat within a few days.

Rhubarb is rich in antioxidants- which protect against cancer.

Rhubarb can be eaten raw- remove leaves, dip in honey or sugar.

Do not plant near tomatoes, tomatoes can damage rhubarb.

To propagate rhubarb, dig out whole root system and divide into sections that each contain new budding plants.

And one last thing- rhubarb, rhubarb, rhubarb, said the expert.

Day Three of EDEN

PEAR

Pear trees don't like cold easterly winds.

It generally flowers earlier than Apple trees.

Conference Pear is best suited to British climate.

Cut unripened full-size pears and leave at room temperature for two days before eating.

Pear trees need another pear tree nearby to pollinate.

Pear trees are bigger than apple trees, and need sun, perhaps on the South side of the Churchyard, but watch those cold winter winds.

Cuttings are easy- take cuttings from new growth in Summer, about a foot long, leave top leaves, remove bark from bottom four inches, dip in rooting hormone, and plant up.

Pears can fruit as quickly as four years.

Where did you plant it ?..
What did you plant ?..
When ?..

BUSH-TUCKER Challenge　　　*13*

Where did you plant it ?..
What did you plant ?..
When ?...

BUSH-TUCKER Challenge

14

Where did you plant it ?..
What did you plant ?...
When ?..

BUSH-TUCKER Challenge 15

Day Three of EDEN

BLACKCURRANT

Blackcurrant bushes can be trained as a hedge, everybody needs a hedge, perhaps to hide the Vicar's new Jaguar, my Dad had one the width of his garden, about six metres long, you couldn't walk through it, it was about five foot high and needed hedge trimming, and bore fruit for us, apple and blackcurrant tarts throughout the summer. It was, I seem to remember, about a metre thick. The excess he gave to family and friends.

Blackcurrant bushes live for up to twenty years.

Do not hoe around the roots, they are fragile and can be easily damaged.

Harvest when fruit is dry and firm, several days after turning black.

Propagating is almost as easy as Strawberry- easier than apple. Wait until leaves have dropped off, cut one foot lengths from new growth, each with a leaf at the top, dip in rooting compound, plant six inches apart, after a year plant out a metre apart.

This is also an opportunity to propagate hundreds of bushes in a few years. Possible income source.

Blackcurrant is full of antioxidants, anticancer, anti-flu, in fact it will keep away almost anything except your auntie.

Day Three of EDEN

STRAWBERRY

When picking fruit, soak the fruit in salt water to remove the fruit fly maggot.

Each of my four strawberry plants had ten shoot runners, which gives you 53,000,000 possible plants after seven years. If each plant gives you ten strawberry fruits, then that is exactly a lot, and puts you in a colossal jam.

The Beatles were right- Strawberry fields forever.

Why not sell the excess plants at Church sales. One million plants at 50p covers your annual Church Share, a new roof, and a bit left over for the Vicar's holiday in Barbados.

To raise new plants from runners, peg down new plants in June-July, using wire hoops, sever about a month later and transplant a week after that, or let run wild in a strawberry patch. I once visited a chap who had a terraced garden, and the whole of one terrace was a strawberry patch, and because it was a terrace, they could be reached from the terrace below. A lot of Church grounds are on slopes, what about a Strawberry terrace.

Strawberries fruit between May and October- except in Torbay, Devon, where I live, because I have a photo somewhere of a strawberry plant with a fruit on it on Christmas day, next to my flowering rose.......

Strawberries aren't as expensive as Raspberries in the shops, but they taste of summer, and they are the easiest to grow, they self propagate, just dig up an area and watch it get covered. They are the perfect food bank fruit, easily picked, a quick wash, and ready to eat.

Where did you plant it ?..
What did you plant ?...
When ?...

BUSH-TUCKER Challenge **16**

Attach PHOTOS

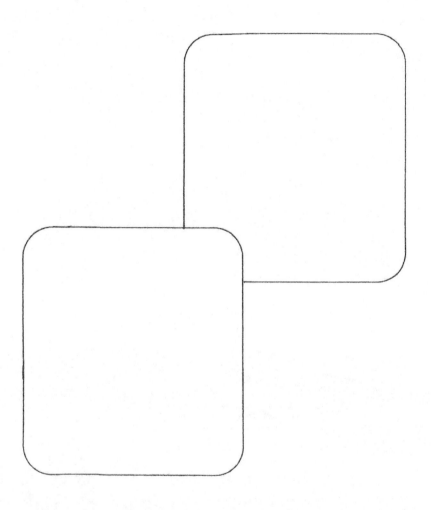

Where did you plant it ?..
What did you plant ?..
When ?..

BUSH-TUCKER Challenge 17

Where did you plant it?..
What did you plant?..
When?...................................

BUSH-TUCKER Challenge   *18*

Where did you plant it ?..
What did you plant ?...
When ?..

BUSH-TUCKER Challenge

19

Stop sitting on the fence
What was your experience like?

Where did you plant it ?..
What did you plant ?...
When ?...

BUSH-TUCKER Challenge **20**

Where did you plant it?..
What did you plant?...
When?...

BUSH-TUCKER Challenge

21

Where did you plant it ?..
What did you plant ?..
When ?...

BUSH-TUCKER Challenge

22

Where did you plant it ?..
What did you plant ?...
When ?...

BUSH-TUCKER Challenge

23

Where did you plant it ?..
What did you plant ?...
When ?..

BUSH-TUCKER Challenge

24

Where did you plant it ?..
What did you plant ?..
When ?...

BUSH-TUCKER Challenge | **25**

Congratulations

on being
Outstanding in your field

and reaching
25

As a Reward, I am happy to illustrate YOUR OWN Home, Shop or Local Public House, worth over £500.

Yours- including research, illustrating, Processing, postage and packing

for only **£99**

Where did you plant it ?..
What did you plant ?...
When ?...

BUSH-TUCKER Challenge

26

Where did you plant it? ....
What did you plant? ....
When? ....

BUSH-TUCKER Challenge | **27**

Where did you plant it ?..
What did you plant ?..
When ?..

BUSH-TUCKER Challenge 28

FREE download of the New Hymn / Anthem for YOUR Church

"This Land of Ours"

A tale of the Christ Child

Music by Colin Gordon-Farleigh, Words by Roger P. Thomas MCSD

Email my studio-
Rogertheartist5@gmail.com

Where did you plant it ?...
What did you plant ?...
When ?..

BUSH-TUCKER Challenge **29**

Where did you plant it ?..
What did you plant ?..
When ?..

BUSH-TUCKER Challenge

30

Where did you plant it ?..
What did you plant ?...
When ?..

BUSH-TUCKER Challenge   **31**

Attach PHOTOS

Where did you plant it ?..
What did you plant ?...
When ?..

BUSH-TUCKER Challenge **32**

Where did you plant it ?..
What did you plant ?..
When ?..

BUSH-TUCKER Challenge

33

ALL the Three's, Thirty Three.
The double 33 offer – 66 reasons to be proud.

Giving it the full lead treatment, I will happily create a pencil illustration of YOUR CHOICE, this is a major piece of work, and will be completed within four months. I can create four of these per year, so get in early as there may be a waiting list.
Normally, the drawing would cost over £500 to complete.
I will then send you the finished artwork for you to frame after I pay for processing scans, up to £100, for it to be made into a Charity print for a HOSPICE of your Choice, up to £4500..
On each print YOUR name will appear as commissioner. This normally costs £150
YOU WILL ALSO RECEIVE Number one in the series, worth £62.

All I require is name of historical building, and to cover processing, research, postage and packing – £66

Kings Arms, Paul, Cornwall

Where did you plant it ?..
What did you plant ?..
When ?..

BUSH-TUCKER Challenge

34

Check out my Celebrity Portraits, over 100 to date, in my FACEBOOK Group

ROGER P. THOMAS MCSD

Where did you plant it ?..
What did you plant ?..
When ?...

BUSH-TUCKER *Challenge* **35**

Where did you plant it ?..
What did you plant ?..
When ?...

BUSH-TUCKER Challenge **36**

EXTRACT from Amazon's

The Eden Godwink

A dozen solutions to the Climate Crisis

By

Roger P. Thomas MCSD

The EDEN *Godwink*

Day Three of Eden

Water is the driving force of all nature
Leonardo da Vinci

The Garden of Eaten

"Take what you need, leave what you can."

The concept is to create a community garden, a growing and free food bank, a provider of Vitamin C, ideally, on Church properties, which is abundant and because the Church has volunteer committees to help with the management and planting of the gardens, they invest their interest and time, and therefore the venture becomes more successful than just employing disinterested people.

I was shocked to learn a few years ago in my research that Seattle was tearing up it's Community Park trees, until I heard the brilliant reason, they were replacing them, even healthy park trees were being cut down, they were replanting areas with fruit bearing trees such as apple, pear and sweet chestnut, these flower and are attractive, and the locals that congregate in these parks, can now benefit from fresh food on their walk, It's so simple and effective.

I wrote to Queen Elizabeth II about twenty years ago and told her she needed to re-afforest the lost areas that Queen Elizabeth I devastated in her ship building efforts, she replied positively, and it was heartening to see the Queen's canopy now underway. Just a few years ago, 2018, I wrote again, saying I had made a terrible mistake, and these trees should not be planted, and perhaps she did not know that every supermarket in her Realm now had a food bank for her starving citizens, and the trees that needed to be replanted should be fruit bearing plants, this time I quoted from Genesis, and also perhaps she could get her Son involved, she wrote back again positively.

I am in the process of writing to my local Council demanding that this concept be considered to make them the most loved and supported Council in the Land, a Beacon and Pioneer for all other Councils, and somewhere the People of Britain would love to live, a World Livability Trend Setter.

Now I understand Africa is to create a Green belt of fruit bearing trees, miles wide and dividing Africa into two, I was heartened. Not just trees but trees with a purpose, however, I now walk through my local parks and am dismayed and troubled, I am like a time traveller, and what would he feel if he came across humans going in the wrong direction, the trees I see, remind me of a Monty Python quote, they are " Nice, but Dim", they could so much be nicer, more productive, more colourful and a partial solution to the spiral we are all travelling downwards.

What of the problems today, they seem insurmountable.

The Covid lockdowns and lay-offs should have taught us that there is no job safe and never again a job for life, anyone anywhere could be living in their car soon, whilst I am writing this India is suffering, and new Covid cases are one third of a million per day, because of the West's greed in looking after number one, we have unleashed a possible ELE, and extinction level event, what if the Covid 19 in the overcrowded and flooded-by-people Indian hospitals changes, and mutates into a killer, more effective that the 5% mortality at the moment, what if it become 25%, that is almost one person in every house across the World, all this because, we look at our individual Countries like Islands, and not a planet, this is a pandemic, not an epidemic.

Britain, particularly and definitely Britain, will be the first to receive an Indian Covid Variant, our population is connected closely to the Indian South Asian continent, closely and effectively. It could happen tomorrow or in a week, what if the new variant was non-symptomatic initially, then when everyone has got it, the variant changes again and attacks the weakened bodies and kills within days, we would have no defence.

Prepare for the worst, hope for the best.

Yes India is also to blame, who the hell thinks that they should have a Space programme, and let's not forget, inoculations and oxygen are manufactured in India and sold to the West.

This is a big problem, and out of our hands, let's count the pennies, and start small by inspiring others to copy.

So what can we do now, locally, that will bear fruit this year, and perhaps turn the corner.

Churches have pretty lawns, and often it is a chore to maintain these by ever more elderly grass cutters, so let's make it easier and more interesting, and a word that I was taught in my twenties, when you have a voluntary job, make it FUN.

Is it going to cost us anything, NO.

Bushes can be donated initially by garden centres, supermarkets, and cuttings from locals, and how about plants purchased with plaques attached, my own Father passed away and has a tree planted at Llangyfelach Churchyard with a plaque, this was twenty five years ago. This is not a new idea, in fact in Celtic tradition, you generally had a tree planted over your grave. I am not suggesting you adopt this, but apple and cherry trees in the graveyard might be a good way to get locals to keep the place tidy, whilst giving Vitamin C to local underprivileged children.

Not so long ago, I experienced poverty, homelessness and hopelessness, instead of bending to the ever powerful dread and blackness, I said to myself, this is being done to me for a purpose, for a reason, this is temporary, I have to learn from the lesson, and when I get into the position to do something about it, I will use all my God given talents to start a change, to put my experiences into something that could either inspire others or actually start to resolve the very problems I was experiencing, learn the valuable lesson I was being taught.

Out of poverty, at the time, to supplement us, I managed to find four sources of free apples within five miles walk of where I happened to be at the time, four old and tired apple trees, accessible, and without getting onto anybodies land, three were clearly trees which had grown from people throwing apples from their car and had grown in hedges on the road side, and twice a week, we had what my wife called comfort food, stewed apples, a few crushed digestive biscuits and cheap sachet of custard on top, twice a week for several months during the apple harvest, occasionally I added a handful of blackberries, I also managed to buy the cheapest roughest porridge, and added a handful of blackberries every morning, what a difference it made.

So what do we need to create this Garden of Eaten, this accessible and free source of fruit, this centre of the community.

As for flowering bushes, I recommend Raspberry, Blackcurrant and Gooseberry. In the ratio 10 : 2 : 1, raspberries are very easy, instantly edible and very very very very expensive. The others are ideal for pie making.

As for trees, Apples and Cherry are the primaries.

Let's introduce some subliminal Christianity, why not use the garden as a base for community events, perhaps a gazebo every saturday morning, raising funds with the sale of Church merchandise, sale of fruit bearing plant cuttings, draw tickets, jumble and books. The Church Magazine, diaries and bookmarks are always popular, it's a meet and greet. The people who you may feel could get embarrassed, might not turn up on

Saturday mornings as this is a fund-raising event, there are six other days for picking fruit, however a noticeboard in close proximity could get the good news message across.

Also a sign must be displayed

TAKE WHAT YOU NEED, LEAVE WHAT YOU CAN
Open to all mankind.

There is also a quote from Genesis 1;29,
" Every tree whose fruit yields seed, to you it shall be for food"

So let's get to the nitty gritty, how can we maintain these plants and get them to increase their yield, and are there any ideas we can use to make their display more attractive and more productive, I have given the rest of the section of this chapter up to one plant per page, beginning with Raspberry and it's cousin the Tayberry, then onto a Blackberry Bramble cloche I designed from an old gazebo.

Onto the staples, Apple, Cherry, Sweet Chestnut, Hazel, Pear, Raspberry, Strawberry and Blackcurrant. Blackcurrant is the perfect hedge, my Dad had a Blackcurrant hedge six foot high and twenty foot long, a perfect hedge for pies, it was for us, and our family and friends, he started an early form of community gardening.

I will also show you the impossible yield, what if you had the space, and the knowledge for cuttings and propagation, strawberries in the right conditions can give you nearly ten million plants in under ten years.

No-one should go hungry, this World can feed the eight Billion ten times over. Did you know a field of grain feeds 98 times a field of Beef, and even in the Bible it says to eat the fruits of the trees and LOOK AFTER, not eat, the animals of the earth.

Here's a frightening fact, how many gallons of water it takes to produce 1lb of food, well it takes 28 gallons for one pound of potatoes, Rice is

164 gallons, Chicken is much more 519 gallons, that is to create 1lb of food, so how much to produce 1lb of beef...One-thousand-eight hundred and fifty one- 1851 gallons of water to produce one pound of food. And here's where it gets even more ridiculous, if you visit any supermarket, it can cost around £3 for a packet of Raspberries, and the cheapest Beef is just £1 a packet. As Spencer Tracey once said... It's a mad, mad, mad, mad world.

So let's begin..........

Nature doesn't need people- people need nature, nature would survive the extinction of the human race and go on just fine, but Human culture, human beings, cannot survive without nature.

Harrison Ford

The Bare Truth-
In a single year over 40 million tonnes of insecticides, herbicides and fungicides are sold in the World- Did you know some insect eating birds consume 100 insects per day.

Where did you plant it ?..
What did you plant ?..
When ?...

BUSH-TUCKER Challenge

37

Where did you plant it ?..
What did you plant ?...
When ?...

BUSH-TUCKER Challenge

38

Where did you plant it ?..
What did you plant ?..
When ?..

BUSH-TUCKER Challenge **39**

Where did you plant it?..

What did you plant?..

When?..

BUSH-TUCKER Challenge

40

Where did you plant it ?..
What did you plant ?...
When ?...

BUSH-TUCKER Challenge

41

Where did you plant it ?..
What did you plant ?..
When ?...

BUSH-TUCKER *Challenge* **42**

Tribute to
DOUGLAS ADAMS
By now reaching

42 on your passport

You now join the
Beer and Peanuts Club,

And to celebrate, I will create a portrait of a celebrity, worth £650, to help facilitate this all I need is basic artwork and research, postage and packing cost, £142 (3 x £47)

Roger P. Thomas MCSD
Official BBC Portrait Painter of Sir Terry Wogan

Your Church could have a similar illustration.

This is a signed and numbered print and comes with a Certificate of Authenticity. These prints can raise up to £50,000 per Church.

To order this print visit
churchprints.co.uk

Where did you plant it?..
What did you plant?...
When?...

BUSH-TUCKER Challenge   43

Attach PHOTOS

Where did you plant it ?..

What did you plant ?..

When ?..

BUSH-TUCKER Challenge

44

Where did you plant it ?..
What did you plant ?...
When ?..

BUSH-TUCKER Challenge

45

Where did you plant it?..
What did you plant?..
When?..

BUSH-TUCKER Challenge **46**

Where did you plant it ?..
What did you plant ?..
When ?...

BUSH-TUCKER Challenge **47**

Where did you plant it ?..
What did you plant ?..
When ?..

BUSH-TUCKER Challenge 48

Where did you plant it ?..
What did you plant ?..
When ?...

BUSH-TUCKER Challenge **49**

Where did you plant it ?..
What did you plant ?...
When ?..

BUSH-TUCKER Challenge **50**

100 yards from a Thatched Inn.

Within 30 miles of your home are a few designed gardens.

Now you have reached **Fifty** fruit-machines and are all fruitful, you will personally receive a signed limited edition print of this Stately Home., the owner's wife was actually the model for the Statue of Liberty, the Ultimate celebrity- just 100 yards from a Thatched Inn, it comes with a certificate of authenticity, and is normally £62. To cover all your pees-processing, postage and packing, just send £20. Non-UK- £30

Where did you plant it ?..
What did you plant ?..
When ?..

BUSH-TUCKER Challenge

51

Where did you plant it ?..
What did you plant ?...
When ?..

BUSH-TUCKER Challenge **52**

AMAZON BOOK SERIES
Be a PILGRIM

New for 2024

Visit Churches as an Ambassador, take back good practice from these Churches, and raise thousands for your own Church

Where did you plant it ?..
What did you plant ?..
When ?..

BUSH-TUCKER Challenge **53**

Where did you plant it ?..
What did you plant ?..
When ?..

BUSH-TUCKER Challenge 54

Where did you plant it?..
What did you plant?..
When?..

BUSH-TUCKER *Challenge* **55**

Win a Limited Edition Print of
"Buddleia"
Signed – numbered and comes with a Certificate of Authenticity
WAS £64

Just ORDER TWO different AMAZON Passports from my range of 300 (Roger P. Thomas MCSD)
Take a photo, hold one in each hand, email to studio

A name will be drawn from the POT.

Where did you plant it ?..
What did you plant ?...
When ?..

BUSH-TUCKER Challenge **56**

Where did you plant it ?..

What did you plant ?..

When ?...

BUSH-TUCKER Challenge

57

Where did you plant it ?..
What did you plant ?...
When ?...

BUSH-TUCKER Challenge **58**

Where did you plant it ?..
What did you plant ?..
When ?..

BUSH-TUCKER Challenge **59**

Where did you plant it ?..
What did you plant ?..
When ?.......................................

BUSH-TUCKER Challenge **60**

Where did you plant it ?..
What did you plant ?...
When ?...

BUSH-TUCKER Challenge **61**

Stop sitting on the fence
What was your experience like?

Where did you plant it ?..
What did you plant ?..
When ?...

BUSH-TUCKER Challenge | 62

Where did you plant it ?..
What did you plant ?...
When ?......................................

BUSH-TUCKER Challenge **63**

Where did you plant it?..

What did you plant?..

When?..

BUSH-TUCKER Challenge   **64**

Attach PHOTOS

Where did you plant it ?..
What did you plant ?...
When ?..

BUSH-TUCKER Challenge **65**

Where did you plant it ?..
What did you plant ?...
When ?..

BUSH-TUCKER Challenge   **66**

Where did you plant it?..
What did you plant?...
When?...

BUSH-TUCKER Challenge **67**

Stop sitting on the fence
What was your experience like?

Where did you plant it?..
What did you plant?...
When?...

BUSH-TUCKER Challenge **68**

Where did you plant it ?..
What did you plant ?..
When ?..

BUSH-TUCKER Challenge **69**

Where did you plant it ?..
What did you plant ?..
When ?..

BUSH-TUCKER Challenge | **70**

The AMAZON Book which unlocked the 30,000 year mystery— was the EARTH Terraformed?

"The Hand of God is all over this"

4444

By
Roger P. Thomas M.C.S.D.

High in the Amazon Book charts for Paranormal literature.

AMAZON SERIES
BE in with

THE INN CROWD

To BEER or not to BEER, that is the question, whether it be you stopping WINING or DINING. Just fill in the passport, raise funds for the local Hospice and get YOUR Local PUB drawn and painted, ooo aarh....

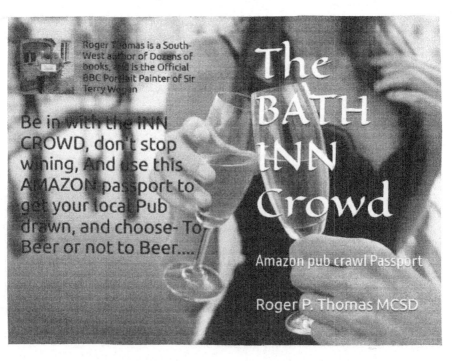

Amazon Book Series

MIND Your MANORS
Roger P. Thomas MCSD

Visit Castles, Manor Houses and Stately Homes, and filling in your passport, even get a painting of your own home

Join the
INTERNATIONAL
HUG in a MUG Club

Visit Cafes and join the Quest for the perfect Roast.
NEW AMAZON SERIES
There is a HUG in a MUG Club for EVERY CITY in the WORLD
Along Your Journey raise funds for the Local Hospice and even get a painting of your own home

AMAZON SERIES

BEAN there done that.

Visit different cafes and establishments on your Quest for the perfect Roast, and raise funds for the Local Hospice as you get your passport stamped, and even get a painting of your own home along the Journey.

Roger Thomas has written dozens of books, a columnist for the London Retired Magazine, and is the Official BBC Portrait Painter of Sir Terry Wogan.

This Amazon Passport challenges you to join the Hug in a Mug Club, and even get your own house painted along your journey...

London Coffee Passport

BEAN there, done that

Roger P. Thomas v.CSD

*Other Books
planned in the Series*

*Wales   England
Scotland
N. Ireland   France
Italy
Spain   America*

All Great Britain's Shires.

Profile

Roger P. Thomas MCSD, has lived in Paignton, Devon for over forty years and has been influenced by the local environment and clean air, he qualified as a Technical Illustrator with Diploma membership to the Society of Industrial Artists and Designers, and City and Guilds in Technical Illustration in 1978 from Swansea Art College, now Swansea University.

Many years at Centrax established him locally as an industrial artist, and when Centrax imploded, he illustrated books for David & Charles, and others such as Webb and Bower, and Letts study Aids. And was at one time the Herald Express Commercial advertisement designer.

As a freelance artist, he has had many solo Portrait Exhibitions, two in London, one at the Royal Commonwealth Centre, he is the official BBC Children in Need portrait painter of Sir Terry Wogan, and has worked with Celebrities across the World, from film stars Tippi Hedren and Dale Robertson in America, to Katherine Jenkins, Russell Watson, Hayley Westenra and Phillip Schofield. Placido Domingo loves the portrait he completed of him. One of the current portraits he is working on, is with the niece of local footballer Justin Fashanu, a tribute portrait. Other agreed projects are Frank Bruno and the Scarlets Rugby team.

He is also managing a project to raise funds for every Church in the UK, through a concept backed initially by Michael, Bishop of Exeter.

As a freelance writer, he has written over half a million words for newspapers, in Devon, Wales, Scotland and Ireland, and magazines such as the Retired Series and Devon Life.

He has supplied over one thousand illustrations for Local, National and International newspapers.

He is a published poet. During Covid lockdown, he started to complete projects that were in his "to do" list, his first book- The Eden Godwink" is an Amazon book, showing the whole World how to reverse Global Warming within seven years, and most importantly not to leave anyone behind, so everyone on the planet has a better life, from the farmer in Bangladesh whose farm is being threatened by being washed away, to the multi millionaire that doesn't want to traipse cables to his car to charge it up, life can improve for everyone, the alternative is hundreds of millions dead across the Globe, and Britain in an Ice Age, one chapter is how every Parish in the South West can lift up the spirits and bodies of the homeless, who tonight will have nowhere to call home, and their children that might not have any Vitamin C through poverty. His local Church is already in the design stage with cutting the sod due next month. This scheme is supported by the Archbishop of Canterbury's office.

His second book- 4444 The Godwink Codex, has just been published by Amazon, showing that Genesis was a failed experiment.

Roger recently represented Paignton at the Devon Climate Change Assembly.

With thanks to Lauren and Kyle
For the idea they planted
of using my very own concept.
A concept I suggested to
Monopoly all those years ago,
of thematizing their game.
My Amazon book "Be a Pilgrim"
should also be converted to
visiting Stately Homes. xx

Also my thanks to Gemma
at Paignton's Axworthys
for reformatting and processing
this manuscript.

Printed in Great Britain
by Amazon

56782478R00066